Gallery Books
Editor Peter Fallon
HARMONY (UNFINISHED)

Grace Wilentz

HARMONY (UNFINISHED)

Gallery Books

Harmony (Unfinished)
is first published
simultaneously in paperback
and in a clothbound edition
on 17 October 2024.

The Gallery Press
Loughcrew
Oldcastle
County Meath
Ireland

www.gallerypress.com

*All rights reserved. For permission
to reprint or broadcast these poems,
write to The Gallery Press:*
books@gallerypress.com

© Grace Wilentz 2024

The right of Grace Wilentz to be identified as Author of this Work has been asserted in accordance with Section 77 of the Copyright, Designs and Patents Act 1988.

ISBN 978 1 91133 890 1 *paperback*
      978 1 91133 891 8 *clothbound*

A CIP catalogue record for this book
is available from the British Library.

Harmony (Unfinished) receives financial assistance
from the Arts Council of Ireland.

Contents

PART ONE
  Home House *page* 13
  The Forty Foot 14
  Shadowboxing 16
  Hospice, New York City, 1995 17
  On Hanging Up My Waitressing Uniform 18
  Glass Frog 20
  A Lean Year 22
  Blush on the Pear 23

PART TWO
  The Charm 27
  Gift of the Magi 28
  I Married You 30
  Washing the Horse 32
  The Artist Fish 33
  Caatinga 34
  Roça 36
  Beaches, Then and Now 37
  Past Imperfect 38
  Interior with Girl Reading 39

PART THREE
  A True Record 43
  Young Rose 44
  In Which My Dad Teaches Me to Throw a Punch 45
  The Harmony Unfinished 46
  Lascaux 48
  Memento Mori 49
  Patience and Order 50
  Terme di Saturnia 51
  Naming the Foals 54
  A Walk in the Woods at Marlay 55
  One for Sorrow, Two for Joy 56
  Elizabeth Bishop's Stove 57

Acknowledgements and Notes 59

Why not the life?
                — *Jack Gilbert*

PART ONE

Home House

Some people have a place they call a 'home house'.
Once I had one too.
I went to yours for the first time
where the kettle boiled steadily
through the mild panic of late for work,
late for the school run.
A feverish child was placed into my arms.
I wasn't sure if I knew how to hold him
but he looked at me with glassy eyes
and, closing them, slept heavy.
I couldn't move. I stayed there for two hours
as family came and went. A meal was cooked,
the extension surveyed and resumed
if only for a little while. The sun
rose higher over the patchwork fields
before dipping low. The day went on
as the days go on. On and on.
I remembered being here — what I mean is a pace —
I was never here before, of course.
What I mean is being in a home house of my own.
Here, on the inside, you don't look out,
don't have time, the way looking in you do.
My arms were like a circle. I sank into the sofa
and the small weight of the boy in my lap
became a part of me until I didn't feel him anymore,
or the holding. I found I could support another
naturally and was surprised when he awoke,
with a bit more life now, able to walk himself
back up the field beside his mother.

The Forty Foot

Each time the sea licked the step
the cold shocked me to my core.
(Worst where the breeze stung my wet skin.)
Another swimmer joined the queue behind me,
and before me it was now just the sea.

Sure, I'd had my day in the Convention Centre,
waited on the labyrinth of snaking queues,
arriving eventually at M–Z. I received the packet
with the certificate, 'Amhrán na bhFiann' photocopied,
a slip for the passport office and the little tricolour badge.

My partner left to sit with the other guests.
We were strange by then, having come apart just as the stress
of whether I'd be able to stay was finally lifting.
A month before he took a day off work to lie for me
at the GNIB office, so I could get my last stamp.

Separated into tiers we sat nervously
while the Garda Band hammed it up with pop songs
until eventually the Minister came out.
And though I'd cried as a guest at my friend's ceremony,
knowing what it meant to her to have her status not tied

to a husband who tried to run her over twice,
when we got to the part where we all sing
'Amhrán na bhFiann' I couldn't understand why I didn't
    feel a thing,
though the eyes of the man from Sierra Leone to my left
and the eyes of the man from the Philippines to my right

were glassy and wet. I knew without looking
that the swimmers queueing behind me were surely
becoming impatient, so I dove. All in, I didn't know

if I was paralysed or revitalized, or how
I'd ever draw a breath again.

But in that cold, opaque sea, somehow I started
treading water and, hand on heart, I never felt so Irish.

Shadowboxing

Is it cage or compulsion?
I feel I've been here forever, swinging,

perpetually in training for meeting
what seeks me out in other realms.

I shuffle or dive and my opponent
falls to pieces of shadow.

Drawing a breath before the bell,
the ring ropes, like all lines, end in shadow too.

Caught cold in a combination, someone
calls 'break', but this brawler, faded,

shady, sticks to me like glue.
Is it consciousness or craving

that I long for, an unreal thing
hidden beneath my shadow?

I have my suspicions about why it resides
there, why I need the shadow,

even as I hang on in a canvas ring,
set deep in an unreachable region.

Hospice, New York City, 1995

It was New York City in the mid-1990s.
It was winter and then spring as we moved through
the palliative care and pain management floor
from the room where my father lay dying,
a pulled yellow curtain his only privacy,
to the office of Bob the social worker
who had come to understand something almost ineffable.
I say almost. He explained it to my mother once
when they were alone together, though I sat there too.

Bringing my father home, and back again to hospice,
beat out the rhythm of our days that were also full
of hour after hour of watching him sleep. A morphine wall
dividing our worlds for the most part. Though there was
one lucid moment when my father asked me to sit
beside him, looked me in the eye and said he hoped
I knew he loved me and my mother very much.
I wondered was it Bob who'd gotten through.

When did I know the meaning of the words that passed
between Bob and my mother, that for all he gave of himself
Bob might not be seen to so tenderly when it came time for him
to wear the thin gown and pass his days in a hospital bed
like so many young men in New York in the mid-90s,
in a city that has forever been two cities,
like life and death, richer and poorer, seen and unseen,
one city lit, the other hidden in plain sight.

On Hanging Up My Waitressing Uniform

They called me blue stockings
because I had thoughts and said them out loud.
Truth is, in a way I loved it:
the sweetness of keeping your eye on someone,
the regulars, the endless chats,
the woman from Irishtown who married a man
from Sandymount, ate alone
until her two boys would be chased out of the park.
Moping beside her they'd brighten to ask:
do ya tink we're good!? And I always did. Because
they were and are. I wasn't
always the best at remembering to watch the hatch,
or hoovering the booths,
but I let people guess my accent as if it were a game.
One day I spelled 'forest'
wrong on the chalkboard dessert menu and laughed
so hard I cried.
I liked seeing the same faces day in and day out
but one morning I had to fly home
after news that my grandmother was in trouble.
And by the time I returned
you could've fit two of me in the black jeans
I'd worn as a uniform,
could've told me I'd never amount to anything
and I'd have believed you, still,
when I unzipped the suitcase I'd left behind
I held the canvas apron
with 'Heineken' embroidered on the pocket,
ran my fingers over
the stitched lettering and thought of the money
and the routine.
I put the apron to one side with the things to keep,
then moved it
to another pile of things to donate, before moving it
back again to keep.

But when I filled up the bin bag for the charity shop
on impulse
I stuffed the apron, two pairs of black jeans, three black shirts
down deep
and deleted the boss's number from my phone,
telling myself,
there'd be something else for me next,
there had to be.

Glass Frog

What good is it,
being this clear,
armour-less, all

spongy heart
beating in
a brittle cage?

Don't say
it's evolution. You
have to live

in your own skin,
sure, but can't you
hide? You with

your delicate
viscera
lit through.

Every animal
in the forest
can smell fear.

No need
to display
a racing pulse

furiously tapping
in search of an exit.
Transparency

is one
of those things
that at first heals

before it binds you,
then uproots you.
You with your

soft edges, you
looking not at all
made for this world.

A Lean Year

Where the winter lifted early I woke
to birdsong and empty streets
like a summer only I could inhabit.

When I thought I could no more be surprised
the dreams started to arrive —
different cities every night.

Thursday, I picked over trinkets
at the Turkish Market in Berlin,
Sunday, sipped espresso

and pulpy juice at a beach bar in a Lisbon
suburb, idling by the glittering Atlantic.
In a shoebox room in a London hotel

I wasted a Saturday night on my belly, writing,
feet resting on the leather headboard
under a mirrored eight-pointed star.

I rose without an alarm to those places
receding but with me still, capped
thermos coffee hot, wrapped sandwiches

for eating between rocks at the Forty Foot.
I cycled along the Grand Canal that proved
it could, in the absence of people, cars,

turn its waters crystal, sustain lily pads
wavering up from the silty bed
to bloom fuchsia. You could say it was

a lean year, even if there was a kind
of plenty too. One of those plague years
we pledge to move on from, and forget.

Blush on the Pear

I'm drawn by the perfect blush on the pear.
On her light feet the dog trails as I go into the kitchen.
She follows each movement as I hold the fruit,
begin to slice it. I eat and offer her a taste.

She looks up at me sweetly, asking for more, and more again.
I've given her nearly half, eat the last and leave her to lick
 the dish.
Tonight the moon waits, concealed in cloud.
Venus seems to be winking at me from the night sky.

PART TWO

The Charm

I arrive at the end of the year,
anxious, exhausted,
power trammelled.

He makes a bath for my feet,
rubs at my calluses
with *le petit remède*.

I breathe deeply and wonder —
just when did my skin become
as hard as my mother's?

He prepares a pitcher of water
steeped with common rue, 'rue' from
Greek *rhutos*, meaning shielded.

Once it has cooled I let it wash over me.
Green leaves stick to the tiles
and I come to bed laughing.

Gift of the Magi

Waking with the tip of my nose
so close to a soft neck
with its delicate ridge of spine —
an ellipsis, a dotted line,

carefully I crawl over and out of bed,
step to the bathroom where I meet
my blanket-creased face and feel
the heaviness of last night's sleep,

and another sensation, too —
as if I have lived a thousand lives
and in this one somehow forged
something beautiful out of a lot of bad luck.

It's my turn to make the coffee,
toast bread and melt cheese.
I open the window to get a read
on the day, lean into the air.

It's almost Christmas though being
from the North you mightn't know it
by the downpours and the heat
already rising from the concrete.

But tonight, between late evening and dusk
(call it *crepúsculo*), lights will come on,
pink and green lining the windows
of the highrises at the favela's outskirts.

At that hour I'll find myself here again
as we make dinner side by side, a song
quietly playing in the background,
chopping beside steaming pots

of rice and beans and sharing a cool beer,
separating spinach leaves, the fresh
from the wilted, patiently waiting
for the bay leaf's slow, certain yield.

I Married You

I married you in a sweaty samba
under fairy light-draped trees in Ibirapuera Park
on a Saturday morning walking hand in hand on The Worm.

I married you outside the club where we sat
under a tree smoking while we watched brothers
fight it out in the gutter on Christmas morning.

I married you in a taxi back from the *festa*
and again days later on the roof of the Martinelli Building,
the whole articulated city before us.

I married you beside a seemingly endless beach,
in an empty bus on a rainy night while we waited for the
   cops to arrive,
and later in a hostel with nothing but the clothes on our backs.

I married you on a sixteen-hour bus journey
as the land turned from tarmacadam and dust to clay,
the plastic cups of coffee growing darker, sweeter with
   each stop.

I married you sharing a meal from one large plate.
I married you after all the dishes had been cleared,
over another glass of beer by the open window.

I married you in the liquid dark of an old *quilombo* at night
amidst the sweet smell of rotting mangoes, fallen,
as the dogs barked warnings to signal the scentless *onça*
   prowling near.

I married you under *via lactea* and the halo
of the ring surrounding the moon which I'd never seen
   before

though I'd been looking at the moon for the whole of
   my life.

I married you asking, Tell me one happy memory.
And you married me saying, Back in the city,
at the window, watching the neighbours' chickens with you.

Washing the Horse

We come in from the field,
as the shadow of a visitor
crosses the kitchen.
His horse stands tied
by its reins to the fence
in the acerola's shade.
When we lift our hands
the horse turns away,
does not know us
by our scent.
We take the lump
of handmade soap,
untie the horse
and together lead him
down to the river,
past the dents
in the sandy yard
where the farm dogs
dug their beds.
We pass through
the quiet buzz
of late afternoon
and reach the river
where the horse hesitates.
We lift the saddle
and lower it to the sand,
take the reins
and gently lead him,
cup water in our hands,
run it over his shining back,
lathering and washing
broad, weary muscle
under bristly coat.
A tired horse patient
in a running stream.

The Artist Fish

We sit in our underwear in the December heat
flipping channels, past *Gazeta*, *TV Cultura*,
pausing as the screen goes aqua
and a pearly fish enters the frame.

We follow the delicate sheen of him
as he darts between weeds, hovers
and waits. The camera moves
to show what he has found: a clearing.

He might be hiding, but no, he drops
to the sea floor and begins to shake,
propelling himself against the sand
wriggling out a furrow. Could he be dying

or just mad? He darts right, then left,
scoots on his belly and flails his fins,
picks up and dives again. Slowly
the camera pans higher to reveal it:

the intricate mandala he's made.
It's like a ship's wheel or a rose unfurled,
or a ruined temple in a submerged city
lit by refracted sunbeams. Then,

from between the weeds, another tiny fish
pokes her head out. She has perhaps
hovered nearby this whole time, now swims
neatly to survey this fresh work.

She floats and dips to inspect a ridge
so close she might disturb its delicate composition
but she is careful, and she turns to join him
before the pair suddenly lift, swim off together.

Caatinga

Like a forest in reverse,
all roots and no crowns,

looking at the oldest biome
is like looking at the past.

Some grasses take centuries
to mature. The interactions

between elements leading here
can't be replicated

in a nursery or a lab. What's
needed is sunlight focused

through cloudy crystal,
overheating drying grass.

Some seeds need fire
to germinate. Some seeds

need to be swallowed.
The fox, the maned wolf,

the bush dog all roam here,
a magnetism in their fur

throwing sparks so all
the dry grasses can be replaced.

Natural fire licks clean
so the new can sprout again,

so the soil can be kept poor,
after all, it was from poor soil

that the Caatinga flourished.

Roça

We should know the names of trees.
Not our names for them
but the names they give themselves.

In their shade the chickens and the horse
are friends; we know because
they gather round his hooves.

If you shine your lantern
on the pen at night you'll see
the pigs embracing in their sleep.

There is a river that runs
behind the farm whose sand
gives way beneath our feet.

There is a river that runs
under the river, so we wade
into it on light feet.

One evening, holding hands
in the running current,
we saw the moon rippling,

small and brilliant downstream.
It waited to rise up between
the trees, take its place

in the night sky. That night we saw
the moon is born in the river.

Beaches, Then and Now

Umbrellas still bloom solid yellow,
sherbert orange, dingy white.
The water is still cloudy and opaque

at the public beaches. Aeroplanes
still fly low, towing banners
advertising: painters, movers,

a Paul McCartney concert.
Time only moves forward
but somehow returns me

to those childhood beaches.
I know I have grown,
but am still tiny in the sea,

and by its measure hardly changed.
Except that now I know
how to keep my feet mostly planted,

resisting the undertow's
familiar tug; also, how to dive
through the unexpected wave.

Past Imperfect

I used to miss
that first morning light
and respect my tears
more than my laughter.

I used to apologize
when I wasn't sorry
and make up other people's
excuses for them.

It used to be possible
to separate me
from my sense of self,
like a shadow peeling away.

I used to live life like a sentence,
diminishing drop by drop,
pretending not to know
that time is king.

Interior with Girl Reading

after the painting by Henrique Bernardelli

Like a last song, this quiet moment,
where one high window filters
light to four near walls —

here is the dream, elapsed.
From creased sheets
yesterday's lines

sing with clarity
as set down by a mind
that hungered for silence.

Days measure themselves
in dutiful working hours
but here and there

one may be stolen back
and lost again in entering
this most private chapel.

As she reads the syllables
are working out their elegant order.
Her pulse is a thick current.

It drowns out the street, the slap
of her sandals falling to the floor,
the water running for the wash

and the steady approach of footsteps
just outside the wooden door.

PART THREE

A True Record

Taller doors, higher ceilings.
Old glass in the windows —
leaded, intricate, detailed work.

Sash windows with their hidden
lead weights perfectly balanced
for the hand to close without strain.

Beams of pitch pine — the timbers
as good as the day they were put in.
No soft wood here.

Blue slates cut from the quarry,
sliced and graded: heaviest
for the bottom, lightest for the top.

Not factory-made from cement,
fibres and adhesives, or finished
with a glaze that will quickly discolour.

No plasterboard, instead lathes of timber,
long, woven with horsehair and skimmed
with a hardened coat. Five days to prepare it.

Once a ceiling is pulled down
no one is going to go
to that bother again.

You see the way things were done
without the tools we have to make the job easier.
The history of the trade is in there.

Young Rose

Young rose, winter is coming,
each petal's soft face a dial.
There'll be another season, sure,
but by then you'll not be found
in the bud, or in the thorn or stem,
but course back into colourlessness
conveying, as the dew evaporates,
to antecedent, sap, for what purpose?
Never again to be as tender bloom.

In Which My Dad Teaches Me to Throw a Punch

It's not often that I'm summoned. Humiliations aren't
   foreign,
and fighting isn't me. But I go along because
I understand him to be resourcing me. I might need this later.

Though he is fallen in his plaid shirt there is a certain grace
as he grows lighter, swifter on his feet. He tells me:
'Make your body an A', and somehow my inner eye

knows exactly what this means. I jump into stance
becoming *A*, first in line in the alphabet, a letter
to give birth to the world. He shows me how to open

my back foot a little, to feel force rising up
from the lower body, as it is rooted. There is a proper way
to make a fist, a correct position for the thumb.

His age-softened palms are my targets. I know
their cool smoothness, and that I must aim well, strike on
   target,
so that I don't hurt him. Every punch I land is a note

in a song. Strung together they form a pattern found
within me. I recognize the rhythm I am punching out:
never wild, never unsteady. My father's palms fly back

with each strike, letting me know that I am gaining strength,
giving momentum, and that the boy on the school bus
who's been giving me shit, now he is really going to fucking
   get it.

The Harmony Unfinished

i.m. Dina Vierny

1

She was a girl waiting,
her red dress, their signal, as she sat in the café
facing the train station, eyes downcast.
Unknown to one another they followed her

at a distance, as she guided a path through the town
and into the mountains, keeping utter silence —
fastidious as the sabbath is kept by some —
in the mountains even a whisper can carry.

2

When she began dozing off while posing
the artist questioned her and she confessed.
The red dress he recalled from painting her.
The only thing to do was to take her

to the mountains, show her the shortcuts
and goat paths of his youth, any known
smugglers' routes. He offered his studio
as a rest stop before the journey on foot

through the Pyrenees to the Spanish border,
before it was closely watched. Up until her arrest
their work continued in the dusty studio, surrounded
by blank-eyed busts, sketches, chipped clay nudes,

dried flowers in jars, preparatory gesso forms,
soft-lipped, poised, marked with hundreds

of tiny crosses to stand sentinel over the people
she would bring in later to sleep on their coats.

The secret police raided her flat on suspicion,
somehow missing the stacks of forged passports,
but imprisoning her anyway. The artist
bartered for her release, and sent her away.

3

In quieter days he worked alone in his studio,
a cinderblock outbuilding dripping with ivy,
dwarfed by her likeness, which he called
not by her name, Dina, nor student nor guide, not model

but 'The Mountain' and, later, 'Seated Bather',
'Air', 'The River'. Then, finally, 'Harmony'
(unfinished) armless, unburdened, a divinity
like mutual benevolence existing outside time.

Lascaux

People try to speak to each other, though through an age.
Crouched low by the fire where earth rules, regulating
movement of water and air. No other light reaches

here, where it is safe to remember in the scrape
of stone abrased or the wet sound of pigment swabbed.
The invention of memory in rock, the hand recording

all that goes on discerning: family, enemy,
friend, who lives on the plains, in the forests,
the marshes, who in the rocks, who can move between.

The meanders of the *Vézère* flow through
limestone cliffs, upstream the land softens
and downstream life flourishes. This black carbon,

this red ochre ground for setting images now faint or already
gone. Such small range of colour from which to voice
out of silence, where even whisper will bounce:

this, the beauty we witnessed galloping through.
This, how hard we fought, and this, who remained.
This, all we lost. And this, how great the beast.

Memento Mori

I idle before a replica of the skull of Lucy,
drawn to her large eye sockets,
sharp cheekbones, broad smile,
once the seat of intelligence,
now a bony case, not an emblem
of poison, death or piracy,
but our indefinitely continued existence.

Time will tell what withstands.
She upright, she only very nearly
human. She life, like an instant
still prevailing, keeper of the record
of change, the longer story
captured in frames, intervals,
what lapses, what adapts.

What am I looking for?
What is she trying to tell me?
That sometimes you can live
forever, just not in the way
that you think? Or maybe
that it's possible to leave something
real — you can leave yourself.

Patience and Order

Her cane rests against the table where she sits
brushing blue cold paint
onto the surface of a piece of glass.

The striations in the first coat fade with the second.
When fired and lit she will have winter blue light
with the silver quality of the waterfall in the distant wood.

The seasons are turning; so is the glass in the fire
where paint slowly fuses to the surface
to be held together with calme. The heart will bind them.

We wait for the slow emergence of her vision —
a window much larger than herself —
revealed to us, piece by bright piece.

She's imagined it completely, sketched out a cartoon
in watercolour, pastel, brush and black ink:
a window to be realized with patient order.

For now, though, the shape of this one piece.
The brush dipped into cold paint, layered and layered again,
each coat deepening into dark indigo, to be blessed with light.

If anyone calls to the studio I'll tell them to return later,
saying, 'Just now Miss Hone is deep in thought,
working on the big windows.'

Terme di Saturnia

These waters you can enter,
even in November,

still wild, still free.
When the people go

the fox weaves through
fields of grain, olive trees,

skirting the pools
that have been flowing for millennia.

Legend has it Saturn,
in a fit of rage

at our wars upon wars,
hurled a bolt of lightning,

split a crater to release
these hot, sulphurous waters.

No lockers in this place
and so I worry for my keys, notebook and pen,

iPhone, bus ticket, dry clothes,
should I be unlucky,

and today be parted from them.
But I've travelled far to get here,

and leaving my bag in sight
ease into the water's heat.

My skin shows the wear of another season,
and the waters bite

at all the ways I believed I had
to become hardened, rough.

I sink deeper and glance at other bathers
who cup their hands, gently lift

water over limb. I am adjusting now,
as how you don't know you're sick

until the cure arrives and you feel
suddenly the mark of miracle.

This is a wild place where the fox
roams at night; there are no gates

to keep her out. What's flowed
for thousands of years still flows

in a gentle pull of water.
Tonight, in a new room, the moon

will pool brightly on the floor
where I climb between clean sheets.

I'll wake with the rough skin
having sloughed off, lifted from me

imperceptibly as I slept. What was I
before? What am I becoming?

A nerve, vein or branch can
present itself again, whole.

This colour, risen on my skin,
is red as lips to speak or whisper,

red like fox hair in the grass
signalling a visitor.

Naming the Foals

It is the darkest time of year in the Northern Hemisphere, months before the growing season, and I am casting about for names.

The birth date is always January 1st. A name must be found before February of the second year. Six names, listed in order of preference, for someone else to decide.

Each name no more than eighteen characters, no initials, no trade names, no numbers — except those above thirty and only if spelled out.

No name that's already in use or that's ever been named. No words like colt or filly. No racetracks or famous winners.

I carry a book for writing down names as they come to me — when pruning back the winter garden, glancing at the clock, pouring a drink:

Sudden Flight, Traveller's Hymn, Blind Faith, Praise the Painter, Second Harvest, Merchant's Dream, Constant Optimist.

A Walk in the Woods at Marlay

Leaves filter yellow light
shining between mossy trunks,
beginning to enter this little copse.

Here the ear of the walker
might share a sound
with the badger, swallow, hare or bee.

Underfoot the seed's destruction
is the green stem sprouting.
New beginnings take shape on the walk.

One for Sorrow, Two for Joy

They say one for sorrow, two for joy,
a decoder for the number
of magpies you might meet on a walk.

The meaning of two birds paired
is simple, like the discovery
of someone infinitely worth loving.

But lately it's one, one, one,
only one that greets you,
startles you in its oneness,

so that in a panic you might
reach for the cool smoothness
of a ring no longer there,

or feel the bright day slip,
like liquid over the lip of a bottle,
as you scan the lawn hoping to spot

that second bird divining joy.
There is only one, like your
reflection in a running stream

not easily bourne away.
And so you curtsy deeply, just
as you were taught, saying:

'Your grace, Your majesty.'
Two for joy, one for sorrow,
one for sorrow, one for sorrow.

Elizabeth Bishop's Stove

Not home, but a symbol of home,
moving from the corners inward
with watercolour and gouache.
It was the free hand chose this
transformer of the dull kitchen
to a warming room, far from
the storm bell's erratic clang.
Too much to lift alone, and yet
it turns up in each new geography —
the wood burning stove in Minas,
the Boston hearth — possible
only in the still moving world.

Acknowledgements and Notes

Acknowledgements are due to the editors of the following publications where some of these poems, or versions of them, were published first: *Banshee, The Cormorant, The Irish Times, Poetry Ireland Review, RTÉ Sunday Miscellany, The Stinging Fly* and *Vox Galvia*. 'Gift of the Magi' was published in *Romance Options: Love Poems for Today* (Dedalus Press, 2022).

The poems, 'A True Record', 'Patience and Order', 'Naming the Foals' and 'A Walk in the Woods at Marlay' were commissioned by Deirdre Black, Heritage Officer at Dún Laoghaire-Rathdown County Council, for *A True Record*, an art book collaboration with photographers Jane Cummins and Aisling McCoy exploring the history of Marlay House in Marlay Park.

Heartfelt thanks to Peter Fallon and the team at The Gallery Press for embracing these poems and for giving them a home. I am grateful to Alexander Rothman for thoughtful feedback in preparing this manuscript, and to Marsha Swan for careful attention to final form.

For space to work and think, my thanks to Keith Payne and Su Garrido for invaluable time in Vigo. To the University of Notre Dame in Dublin — especially Eimear Clowry Delaney and Kevin Whelan — I'm grateful to be the recipient of your inaugural Writer-in-Residence award which helped greatly in getting me through the home stretch of this book. Thanks to Sirius Arts Centre in Cobh for two weeks of quiet by the sea. Finally, my sincere gratitude to the Arts Council/An Chomhairle Ealaíon for the Next Generation Artist Award which supported completion of this work.

> The book's epigraph by Jack Gilbert is drawn from his 2005 interview with *The Paris Review* in which interviewer Sarah Fay asks, 'What, other than yourself, is the subject of your poems?' Gilbert responds by saying, 'Those I love. Being. Living my life without getting diverted into things that people so often get diverted into. Being alive is so extraordinary, I don't know why people limit it to riches, pride, security — all of those things life is built on. People miss so much because they want money and comfort and pride, a house and a job to

pay for the house. And they have to get a car. You can't see anything from a car. It's moving too fast. People take vacations. That's their reward — the vacation. Why not the life? Vacations are second-rate. People deprive themselves of so much of their lives — until it's too late. Though I understand that often you don't have a choice.'

page 14   The Forty Foot is a promontory at Sandycove from which people enter the Irish Sea to swim all year round. GNIB is the Garda National Immigration Bureau.

page 28   *Crepúsculo* is the Portuguese word for twilight.

page 30   This poem owes a debt to Shane McCrae's 'We Married . . . ' poem series from *Mule*, early drafts of which I first encountered when we were in Jorie Graham's workshop together at Harvard. The concept and rhythms have no doubt stayed with me since then and influenced the poem.

'The Worm' is an elevated highway named for the *minhocão*, an earthworm-like creature. *Festa* is Portuguese for party. A *quilombo* is a Brazilian hinterland settlement founded by people who escaped slavery. *Onça* is the Brazilian jaguar. *Via lactea* is Portuguese for the Milky Way.

page 32   Acerola is a small fruit-bearing tree.

page 33   *Gazeta* and *TV Cultura* are Brazilian television stations.

page 34   *Caatinga* is a Tupi word meaning 'white forest' used by indigenous peoples of Brazil to designate dry forests in interior northeastern Brazil. The poem is informed by the research of archaeologist and anthropologist Altair Sales Barbosa.

page 36   *Roça* is the Portuguese word for farm.

page 38   This poems makes reference to song lyrics by Gal Costa and Gilberto Gil.

page 39   'Interior com Menina que Lê', is an oil painting by Brazilian painter Henrique Bernardelli. It is housed at the Museu de Arte de São Paulo (MASP).

page 46   Dina Vierny was a French artist's model who worked for ten years with sculptor Aristide Maillol. After Maillol moved to Banyuls-sur-Mer in 1939, she worked as a guide smuggling refugees out of occupied France during World War II. 'Harmonie', for which Dina modelled, was Maillol's last, unfinished sculpture.

page 49 Lucy or Dinkinesh is the nickname given to the partial skeletal remains of a female of the *Australopithecus afarensis* species. A rare fossil, her discovery provides insight into the story of human evolution.

page 50 Eva Sydney Hone, known to most as Evie, was an Irish painter and stained glass artist. Her windows can be found throughout Ireland, including in Government Buildings and Trinity College Dublin. This poem makes use of terminology from the art of stained glass: a cartoon is a drawing for a full-size stained glass window; metal strips called calme (sometimes spelled calm or came), usually made of lead, are used to hold pieces of glass together; their centre is known as the heart.

page 51 *Terme di Saturnia* is a group of natural hot springs located in the municipality of Manciano in Italy, close to the village of Saturnia.

page 54 This poem is written from the imagined perspective of Philip Love, the last private owner of Marlay House before it was bought by Dublin City Council in the 1970s. He was a market gardener, horse breeder, and one of the largest tomato producers in Ireland. He is most famous for being the owner of the Larkspur which seemingly came from nowhere to win the Epsom Derby in 1962.

page 55 This poem is after the painting by Evie Hone. It reflects the dual influences of her work in stained glass, as well as her cubist style.

page 57 When Elizabeth Bishop purchased her final home at Lewis Wharf in Boston she wrote in a letter to Ilse and Kit Barker that she was now settled because of her Franklin stove. She had one, too, at her home in Ouro Preto, Brazil, as evidenced by a postcard she sent in May 1970 to Marianne Moore. The stove turns up in her paintings, and 'stove' is one of the end words in her poem, 'Sestina'.